*What I Cannot Change*

# WHAT I CANNOT CHANGE

LeAnn Rimes *and* Darrell Brown

**harper**studio

B
RIMES

HarperCollins books may be purchased for educational, business, or sales promotional use. For information please write: Special Markets Department, HarperCollins Publishers, 10 East 53rd Street, New York, NY 10022.

FIRST EDITION

*Designed by Emily Cavett Taff*

Library of Congress Cataloging-in-Publication Data has been applied for.

ISBN 978-0-06-180426-7

09 10 11 12 13   OV/RRD   10 9 8 7 6 5 4 3 2 1

*What I Cannot Change*

*I look like Minnie Mouse with bow ears.*

# My Story

*I never* knew the power of one song. Over the years, I've recorded hundreds of songs. I've put my heart into each of them in a different way. Some have been hits; others, not. You never know how or why a particular song catches on. It's always a mystery to me why certain songs seem to resonate more than others. That is, until I wrote "What I Cannot Change" with my dear friend and songwriter Darrell Brown (you'll hear more from him later). From the beginning I knew there was something special about this song; not just the lyrics but everything about the song. A song can become a hit in many more ways than just money and radio play. For me this song became a hit because I saw—through postings on my website—how the song inspired people to change their lives and reveal deep secrets and also helped them understand the things in life that they can—and cannot—change. Before sharing those stories with you in the rest of the book, first I'd like to share some of the ways this song has helped me grow as a person—both emotionally and spiritually. For me it's about becoming more transparent. Many of these stories and feelings I've never shared before with anyone. But so many of you have taken the time to share your stories with me on the "What I Cannot Change" website that I wanted to open my heart even more.

I grew up in the spotlight, where it can be hard for public perception to grow up along with you. Many people still picture me as the little girl who sang with a big voice on the song "Blue." In reality, there is so much more to me. I was born in Jackson, Mississippi. At age five, I won my first talent contest, and at age seven my parents had me record my first independent album. By then my family and I had relocated to Garland, Texas. My parents knew how much I loved to sing and to entertain, and I got my first break performing on *Johnnie High's Country Music Revue* in Fort Worth, a popular show that features local artists and national acts. It wasn't long before I recorded my second album at the grand old age of eleven. That project featured the song "Blue" and caught the attention of legendary executive Mike Curb, who signed me to Curb Records. By thirteen, I had a national hit. The rest became history. My history. Along the way, the little girl with the big voice has matured into a young woman, married to the dearest person on earth and the love of my life, my husband, Dean Sheremet. We have been married seven years, and I am so thankful we met.

I admit it's not easy to lay my soul bare—for one person to get to know me, let alone the whole world. Yet there's also a beautiful, enlivening freedom in becoming transparent, to being vulnerable. It can be exhilarating and scary all at the same time. I know I'm definitely on the road to accepting myself for who I am. I'm learning to let that speak for

*My mom put me in dance class when I was two years old because I was so clumsy. It helped . . . a little. I look really focused.*

*My grandfather and me. I loved him so much. He would give me a twenty-dollar bill every time my family and I would go home to visit him in Mississippi. He told me to save them all and one day I would be rich.*

itself, learning to love my real emotions and to let those emotions come across in my relationships, in my life, and in my music.

My early life was exciting. I knew I was raised with a lot of love from my parents, but I was also raised with lots of worry and fear: the worry about where money was going to come from, the worry about whether my song was doing well on the radio charts, and the worry about my family staying together.

That was my biggest worry. I constantly worried that my parents were going to split up. There were times when my parents would get into fights, and my father would come so close to walking out the door, and I would cry and scream for him not to.

They had tried for twelve years to have a baby and nothing ever happened. Then one day out of the blue, the answer to their prayers came when my mom found out she was pregnant. For my mom, I was a miracle child. Not only did she finally have a child of her own to love

*My dad was so handsome. I was and always will be a Daddy's girl.*

*This was at a dance competition. I remember hating that outfit because it was so itchy. I'm the blonde on the right.*

and care for, but my father was there by her side. In many ways, I guess I was the glue that kept my parents together. I still feel that the stress of their trying to conceive a child for so long put unwanted pressure on my parents' relationship, making them question even staying together. They did end up staying together for another fourteen years.

Growing up, I was taught to be the best at everything. Whether it was softball, piano, dancing, or singing, I had to be the best. I was taught that if I wasn't the best then why should I be doing this at all? In this way I felt I was robbed of a nurturing development—allowed to just be a kid and be able to make mistakes. Being raised in Texas added to the pressure. As a girl growing up in Texas, it seemed like every day I was judged on how pretty my hair was and how beautifully I dressed. Because of the gift of singing I was given, my family and friends showed me off in any way they could. Now that's not to say that as a child I didn't like that kind of attention—I did. I loved to sing; but looking back I can tell you it was very overwhelming at times.

Looking pretty wasn't always so easy. I was diagnosed with psoriasis—a horrible skin disorder that covered me with unsightly silver-colored scales and lesions. My whole body itched and turned red. Sometimes, I scratched my skin so hard I was covered in blood. For three or four years almost 80 percent of my body was covered like this. I would never wear shorts or short dresses, and my parents made sure my body was covered at all times. For years my parents would apply all these medicines on me every morning and every night. They struggled so hard to find a way to get my psoriasis under control. A lot of the medicines they would apply on me were steroids that would thin out my skin. Sometimes my legs would look so horrible that I would have to wear two pairs of stockings to hide the lesions when I was singing onstage. There would be days when I would come home from school crying because of the awful teasing I would get from kids. They would call me horrible names like "Scaly Girl" and tell everyone I was contagious. I know now it was ignorance. I think this was one of the reasons I hid my emotions so much later on in life. I had been so used to covering myself—both emotionally and physically. Thank

*This is one of my favorite photos of me. My hair was so perfectly straight and blonde. I remember adoring that doll.*

*How proud I was to be graduating from fifth grade.*

*Was there ever a time in my life when I wasn't coiffed?*

*This picture reminds me again how much I adored the Christmas holidays as a kid.*

*I remember thinking I was so sexy in this dress.*

*This was a major milestone in my life. I had always dreamed of playing the Grand Ole Opry. Not only was I living out one of my dreams by performing on the Opry stage, I was also presented with platinum records by the president of my label, Mike Curb.*

God there are better medicines being made currently to help control my outbreaks. But even now when people say I have such beautiful skin, my first reaction is to recoil and hide. I am learning to receive the compliment now, and it feels unbelievable and so healing.

Even with the disease I still felt the pressure to be the best. Because I had to be the best and on display all the time, the joys of my childhood faded and left me frustrated and wanting for something more. It was weird, because as I grew older there would be days when I would wake up and not want to put on a show for anyone, when I didn't want to get dressed and all prettied up for the day and sing. I just wanted to be. That's been the hardest part for me because it always seems like there is a show. But it's funny, when I wasn't putting on a show I didn't know what to do with myself. Who was I without it?

For me, those limitations stopped me from living out some of my dreams and trying new things. And even if I agree to venture into something new, I can't stop worrying about how it's going to look to the rest of the world if I fail. Fear can be crippling. It has been for me at times. Now I am making a conscious effort to push through my fears and take more chances. Yes, I might fail, but that's where I will learn the most. I am learning to trust myself. I am learning to grant myself grace, realizing that this is the best job I can do at this moment in my life. I am also allowing room for enjoyment and to finding joy over and over with my husband and our home, my animals, friends, and of course, my family.

*This was taken at the beginning of the whirlwind of my very early success. We all were exhausted.*

There was little joy when my parents got divorced when I was only fourteen. This was really a hard time for me. I think both of my parents felt that because I was a very strong fourteen-year-old woman-child who was now financially stable from my music career taking shape that the divorce wouldn't be as hard on me. Even I didn't realize how hard it was on me until a few years ago. My mom and dad divorcing had more of a profound effect on me and my heart than I had realized. It left a big hole in me. It left a big hole in all of our lives.

Over the years, the relationship between my father and me became even more strained. You may have read about some of the legal problems in the newspaper. It was a difficult and painful time for all of us. The perfectionist in me so much wanted to control the situation and fix everything, but here again was life at its most uncontrollable. Looking back on this time through the filter of the song, I have come to a new understanding after reconciling with my father. It is good to have my father back in my life again.

I am now trying to rewire my brain to stop thinking "it's the end of the world" thoughts. By opening my heart and trying to pour these

*This was my first band and me taking a photo in front of a congratulations banner on Music Row in Nashville.*

feelings into my work and into my songs as a songwriter, I feel it is propelling my growth as a person. The more I expose myself, the more confident and safe my heart becomes.

My husband, Dean, has changed my heart—and life—in more ways than I can ever imagine. We met in Los Angeles when I was hosting the Academy of Country Music Awards. It was almost an instant attraction. I looked into his eyes and trusted him immediately. Don't ask me how or why. The crazy thing is that at the time it was hard for me to trust anyone, much less someone I had just met. Not only was I struggling with trusting my family and my record company, but as a celebrity, one minute everyone loves you, the next minute they don't know who you are.

But Dean was different, and I knew he was the one for me. A year after that meeting we got married. He motivates me to take care of myself and encourages me to be healthy and happy. He's an amazing dancer and in great shape, so now we exercise and work out together. As for kids, we're definitely thinking about it and have talked about what that life would be like. It's a constant battle in my mind. One minute I think I'm ready and the next minute I want to wait until I'm forty. Whatever we decide, I'm now feeling more comfortable about those things in life that I can change—and those I can't.

I believe that is how the song "What I Cannot Change" was conceived. The song comes from a place where I allowed myself to be vulnerable yet strong at the same time. It's about my learning about forgiveness, acceptance of myself, and a higher will other than my own. It's

*My twenty-fifth birthday party. That cake rocked!*

*Dean and I on the set of my "Some People" video shoot, one of the first songs I ever recorded of Darrell's.*

*(left) I love taking any kind of camera and holding it up and taking a picture of Dean and myself—some of my favorite pictures have come from doing it this way.*

about my understanding of where, when, and how to stand up or not to stand up for myself.

"What I Cannot Change" is one of those songs that, as a songwriter, is a true gift that comes around once in a lifetime. But I cannot take all the credit. I cowrote this song with my amazing friend Darrell Brown, who has helped me through some troubling times in my life.

Over the years, Darrell and I have developed a strong bond that goes well beyond just writing songs together. I remember first meeting him at a Mexican restaurant in Nashville. We met through a mutual friend, and I remember that he had this larger-than-life personality. Although I didn't recall his name after meeting him again six months later, his huge personality stayed with me. I thought to myself, Who the hell is this guy? He would say the most unexpected things, and truthfully I thought he was absolutely crazy. Indeed, I never met anyone like him in my life except perhaps for my husband.

Our strong bond led to us writing many songs together. We collaborated on a lot of the songs on the *Family* album. Darrell has helped me find transparency in my life and become a better songwriter and person. Darrell is someone I truly admire. He is always authentic, especially in his friendships. Knowing Darrell has changed my life forever. He is the big brother I never had and the guiding light in some of my darkest moments. I love him more than he could ever know.

I can trace the inspiration of "What I Cannot Change" to a very dark day in my life. Darrell was there for me when I was trying to figure

*This was my very first photo shoot for my album* Blue. *I remember feeling so cool and terrified all at the same time.*

out how to love myself and how to love the people who were dear to me. I wanted to keep them in my life even though we didn't agree. It's hard to watch the people around you go through life without changing. I was working so hard to change myself for the better, but I felt others weren't. I felt like I was leaving them behind but didn't want to.

I vented all of this to Darrell, and he listened and quietly took notes on everything I was saying. At the time I thought this was kind of strange, but after I got through venting, Darrell told me I had to come over to his computer and look at the notes he had been taking from our conversation. He said that we needed to write a song based on all of these confessions, these unfiltered, honest feelings that we shared together. We put these heartfelt outpourings into verses and we stepped away for a couple of weeks, still not realizing where this song was leading us. Darrell and I got back together after a few weeks, and once again I had an overwhelming revelation: I had to let go of the things that I couldn't change about other people in my life; the things that I couldn't change about myself; and start figuring out how to love myself and other people, even with all their faults. This revelation felt like a floodgate opening up, and emotions were pouring out of me.

At that moment the chorus of the song revealed itself to us as a gentle prayer. It is a prayer I find myself saying throughout moments every day. It gives me a starting place when I am trying to find some simple peace in the midst of my struggles. Maybe that's why it touches people so profoundly and why I've had such amazing feedback from everyone who hears the song.

I first sang the song publicly in Las Vegas at a concert. The morning of the concert I recorded some radio promotions. I sang "What I Cannot Change" in a small room of about twelve people. When I finished singing, I looked around the room. I couldn't believe it. Not only was my manager in tears, but so was the whole roomful of record label executives. Now that's never happened before, and I thought, Wow, this is a pretty powerful and emotional song.

*This was the wedding of my mom and stepfather, Ted. What a beautiful day that was. I was so happy for the both of them.*

I didn't realize the extent of the power of the song until later that night. I was onstage and nearly halfway through my set. I wasn't planning on singing "What I Cannot Change." In a spur-of-the-moment decision, I decided to perform it. Before the concert, everyone had kept saying that I should perform the song, but I still felt like it wasn't time yet. I wasn't ready. There's a difference between singing for a few people and thousands.

As I performed the song, something inside me told me not to look down at the crowd. I had this strange feeling somebody was crying. I could feel it. I knew that if I saw people crying I would lose it too, so I just closed my eyes and sang my heart out. When I finished the song, I opened my eyes. It looked like the whole crowd was bawling as they all stood up. Seeing their reaction made me lose it, too. For a full five minutes I could not stop crying. I cannot tell you how gratifying it was to see people respond to a song like this.

Since that performance I became more and more aware of the magnitude of what had happened—this was a life-changing song. I saw how deeply it was affecting so many people during my concerts. I thought that there must be a universal message here. The song in a way gives people the courage to take control of their lives. As I performed the song more regularly, and with the release of the album, people started sharing their own personal stories. At first the e-mails trickled in, then more and more. I read them with Dean and we decided we wanted a place for everyone to share their stories. So we set up a website for the song: www.whaticannotchange.com.

We decided that this was going to be a place where people could anonymously post their deepest and darkest secrets. There would be no judgments or comments. I wanted this to be a safe haven for people to let go of the things that weighed them down and get something off their chest. Just like writing "What I Cannot Change" was a huge relief and a liberating experience for me, I wanted everyone who heard my song to feel a little freer and say what they needed to say.

The postings were incredible and moving to read. Dean and I stayed up many nights crying over the heartfelt stories people posted and trusted us with. For me, the most interesting postings were the most immediate: A message right after a life-changing event. There is one posting that hit pretty close to home. The writer is a fourteen-year-old girl going through some hard feelings when her family splinters apart. Her feelings of helplessness and heartache from trying to mend her family reminded me of myself when I was her age. There was another writer who at the age of fifteen had been sexually molested by a stranger; she got pregnant, then had an abortion. Then she wrote about a boyfriend who came into her life who would beat her. Her life was spiraling downward with her self-destructive behavior, and then one afternoon she heard "What I Cannot Change" on the radio. She said she just started bawling. Right then she decided to stop making bad decisions for her life and try to forgive herself for everything. While reading this posting it felt like a lightning bolt ran right through to the core of me. I do not know if I would have had the inner strength that this woman has to keep going and not give up.

I was truly humbled by her moving words. I have many gay and lesbian fans, friends, and supporters. After reading another post on the website of a gay man who hopes his sister hears the song and learns to accept who he is, I just immediately sent out a prayer for him and his sister. There are so many more stories here that have moved me, but for now I'll let you find your own inspiration.

*My stepfather, Ted, took this photo of me.*

# DARRELL'S STORY

*Songs* are a collaborative effort. And this song—and book—would not be possible without Darrell. Here's how he remembers our first meeting and genesis of the song.

I first met LeAnn at the Wildhorse Saloon in downtown Nashville in 2000. My best friends brought me that night to watch her film a performance segment for a television show. I so vividly remember LeAnn singing Kris Kristofferson's song "Me and Bobby McGee"—the one that Janis Joplin immortalized in the 1970s. LeAnn sang the song flawlessly three times. Each time I was amazed by her voice. Each time her voice reached new levels of excitement. I will always remember this first impression of LeAnn.

It was some time before I met LeAnn again at a Mexican restaurant for an impromptu dinner with some mutual friends, and even after that we didn't start collaborating as songwriters until the summer of 2004. When we started collaborating, I was again taken aback by how easy the songwriting flowed out of LeAnn. Up until then, other composers wrote most of the songs LeAnn had recorded on her albums, so I had figured she wasn't a songwriter but was more of a performer.

As LeAnn and I started writing together, I found us connecting almost immediately on a lot of levels. Inside of her were a timeless voice and a hidden talent for songwriting. We felt safe both emotionally and spiritually together. In many ways, songwriting can be like a group therapy session. Our conversations about all the ups and downs in our lives would naturally find a home in our songs. LeAnn would lay bare in our writing her fearlessness and vulnerability. I'm so grateful for that openness. If it weren't for that, there would not be a "What I Cannot Change" song in our lives.

One evening LeAnn and her husband came over to my house for dinner. As it happened, LeAnn had been having some family issues. She told me it had been a weird and emotionally cathartic week for her. Coincidently, I was going through a similar experience myself. Our similar circumstances led to a conversation about letting go of people and things in our lives that we have no control over. It felt more like therapy, but I'm no therapist. I'm a songwriter.

Throughout our conversation, I felt inspired to start typing out phrases and word groupings of some of the heartfelt things that LeAnn shared with me. This annoyed her a bit since she thought I wasn't really listening to her. I told her I was and started reading back some of the ideas we discussed. Her eyes lit up like fire.

What happened next surprised me even more. Immediately, we started arranging the sentences and phrases into couplets, and then arranging the couplets into verse order. A song was in the making! The mood of our conversation was still hanging heavy in the air, so I started playing chords and playing with melodies, and the verses started to naturally fall into place. All of the verses came out in that one moment. We had no idea what the title of the song would be or what the chorus would sound like. We just let it be. We did not want to force the song. We stopped for the evening and went upstairs and joined Dean and my partner, Roger, for dinner.

A couple of weeks later LeAnn and I started talking about how we had survived our last personal battles. Peace was returning to our lives, and we started comparing notes about how we survived our family and work issues from the weeks before. Again we both came to the realization about how little control we have over people, places, and things in this life other than to say a prayer about letting go and simplifying life.

Of course, like most songwriters our thoughts went back to our unfinished song—the verses we had written and the missing chorus. We understood now. This song was going to be a prayer—for us! Within minutes of that realization, the chorus started to gel. We talked more about letting go, forgiveness, and love. As strong-minded artists, we also believed that some things are meant to change, but only if we are brave enough to try to take a stand for that change. How can we have the chorus of the song reflect both sides of our hearts?

I was amazed again by what can happen creatively between two people who trust each other. We wrote a beautiful chorus, and the melody floated and spun in the air around our heads.

We knew that this was a song about how our lives had changed and about the people around us who we couldn't change. It had to be called "What I Cannot Change." This was a song about the vulnerability to allow change to happen, the courage it takes to ask for change, and the almighty grace it takes to trust and accept whatever the outcome will be.

To be in a room with LeAnn, who is willing to be so honest with me. To be in a room with a friend you love and who loves you back with the same abandonment and conviction. To lean on each other's trust as we do. This song needed our willingness, our honesty, our love, our conviction, and safety to be birthed. Not one word or melody would have come down to us to sing or play without that 100 percent commitment between us. We both know that neither one of us would have written "What I Cannot Change" alone. I know I'm a better man and songwriter because of LeAnn's friendship and trust. This song is now my own personal serenity prayer, and I am forever grateful.

# Some Final Thoughts from LeAnn

*I remind* myself constantly that things don't only change by putting my shoulder to the stone and rolling troubles back up the hill. Change can profoundly take place in my life with patience and love. By taking a stand either alone or with my husband or with a friend. Change can take place with prayers and meditation, and more important, things can even change without my lifting a finger or saying a word. I am learning that change can take place without my being a superhero. That is a hard lesson to learn, not to do anything and actually let change happen in its own special, transforming, miraculous way.

There is forgiveness that I thought would be the hardest part of life . . . like forgiving someone for an unjust wrong—or even better, trying to receive someone else's forgiveness that they are wanting to give me. But I discovered that learning to love what I cannot change is one of the most difficult challenges in my life. Learning to love any kind of loss, hurt, or divorce—these things have changed me in the deepest places. But I believe that new life rises out of these shattered places. So I hold on to that little sliver of hope every day. Like a flower pushing its way through the concrete sidewalk, I am now learning to welcome the blossoming.

After Darrell and I wrote this song, and I started performing it, I had no idea what kind of floodgate of public emotion we had opened. Through other people's stories we all can see that we are not alone. We are struggling with the same issues and problems. After reading through many postings on the website, we decided to collect them and divide them into themes: Depression, Faith, Sobriety. . . . As you read, you'll see that these themes are more fluid. Whatever the category, I think these sto-

*I was fourteen years old when this photo was taken of me performing at a July 4th concert in Garland, Texas.*

ries tell us something about ourselves. Despite our different experiences in life, we are all just the same. We are all struggling with some of the same things in life, and I hope these stories help you realize that you are not alone in the things you cannot change. "What I Cannot Change" is the most special song that I've ever recorded, and I hope it continues to touch everybody. I hope this song touches you. I hope the website touches you. I hope this book touches you. That's what this song is all about.

## What I Cannot Change

*I know what makes me comfortable*
*I know what makes me tick*
*And when I need to get my way I know how to pour it on thick*
*Cream and sugar in my coffee*
*Right away when I awake*
*I face the day and pray to God I won't make the same mistakes*
*Oh the rest is out of my hands*

*I will learn to let go what I cannot change*
*I will learn to forgive what I cannot change*
*I will learn to love what I cannot change*
*But I will change, I will change*
*Whatever I, whenever I can*

*I don't know my father*
*Or my mother well enough*
*Seems like every time we talk we can't get past the little stuff*
*The pain is self-inflicted*
*I know it's not good for my health*
*But it's easier to please the world than it is to please myself*
*Oh the rest is out of my hands*

*I will learn to let go what I cannot change*
*I will learn to forgive what I cannot change*
*I will learn to love what I cannot change*
*But I will change, I will change*
*Whatever I, whenever I can*

*Right now I can't care about how everyone else will feel*
*I have enough hurt of my own to heal*

*I will learn to let go what I cannot change*
*I will learn to forgive what I cannot change*
*I will learn to love what I cannot change*
*But I will change, I will change*
*Whatever I, whenever I can*

*Forgiveness*

*I* will learn to let go of the marriage I was unable to keep together. I will learn to forgive the woman who took that away from my children and me.

I will learn to love and trust people again.

I will learn to be strong for my family and move forward, giving my kids all the love I can, and learning from my mistakes.

Thank you for writing this song. It makes people think and overcome the sorrow and difficulties in their lives.

I'm twenty-two and a mother of three, and I will learn.

---

*I* will learn to let go of the hurt and anger my ex-husband's drug addiction has caused our children and me. I will learn to let go of the painful past. I will learn to keep my eyes forward and my heart in the present. Over the years I have learned that I cannot change my past no matter how much I have been hurt. My father took my family from me and for so long I hated him. I still do sometimes. But I think I have finally come to a place that allows me to live without him and without the memories. I've taken so many steps to get here, and I think it's taken more than I thought I had. More than I thought I could give or had left. However, I feel I have succeeded, and I don't think I'll ever deal with what he did to my mother or me ever again. I forgive him and myself.

*I* do forgive you, Mother. I feel that I am a better person now after seeing the mistakes and hard life that you had to live because of the choices you made. I am now grateful for that. I do have some fond memories, but other memories as well. And I thank God every day that I've been able to grow and truly forgive and move on with my own life. I'll always have a warm place in my heart for you, and I'm so sorry that your life was so difficult. I do love you.

---

*T*he first time I heard this song, I spent the rest of the day crying. It felt so much like what I was feeling. I grew up in a very bad environment where my father was controlling. He was physically, mentally, and emotionally abusive to my mother. I kept it a secret until I met my husband; he was the first person I told. I have continued to have a tough relationship with my parents, especially my father. Nothing I do is right for him. Through counseling I have started the process of healing and forgiveness, but it is not easy. So when I heard this song, I really felt connected to it. I really hope others listen to this song and realize that from struggle comes strength.

*W*hile listening to the track recently, I came to a realization about my mother and me: I don't know my mother as well as I should, nor does she know me that well. It was so upsetting to me that the lyric "I don't know my . . . mother well enough" made tears run down my face. I wish I could change this, but I just don't know how. I'll just have to let go or find a way to make it happen. I have to learn to forgive and be forgiven.

———

*A*t the age of seven my parents were divorced. My mother was cheating on my father. And my father was verbally abusive and had a very short temper. My mom had a drug addiction problem and also was an alcoholic. She was always in trouble with the law and spent most of my youth in prison. My father raised my two younger siblings and me on his own. He worked nights mostly so I had to look out for my siblings a lot. I matured very quickly because my mother was never there and my siblings looked up to me. I helped them with their homework and looked out for them in school. I basically helped my father raise them. My dad had such a short temper that he would verbally abuse us a lot. I stuck up for my siblings and was hit several times by my father for it. When I was about fourteen, I realized my mom made a lot of unkept promises and only contacted me when she wanted help with money or something. My dad would exaggerate the way my mother was and told me I would be just like her. After two years without speaking to my mother, and excluding her from my graduation, I learned to forgive her but still be cautious. I also learned to forgive my father and try to get along with him.

---

My father is gay and I was okay with that, it didn't bother me. When I was younger, I was Daddy's little girl. As I grew older I learned that he wasn't paying child support and was trying to take my mom to court and take money from her while she was caring for my brother and me by herself. My father grew to be a selfish man, and we would only hear from him when he wanted something. He did things for himself and rarely others. During this time he started looking unhealthy, and we learned that he had AIDS. I still loved my father even though he was gay and with AIDS, but the man that he was becoming was not a good person. I no longer talk to my father because of the way he has become. I oftentimes blame him for the way I am now and the things I go through. My mom has always told me that I need to forgive him and find some way past it. I have tried, and it always seemed hard. I always wondered what I would do if he died. I'm learning to forgive him and move past this.

---

When I was young, I had dated a guy through junior high school and high school. Later I found out he had lied to me through the years about using drugs. After that, I dated another man who I thought I knew until he showed me his true colors. Now, I'm happily married to my hero. He's my hero because he listened to me and was always there for me. Now we've been married for twelve years and have a wonderful son. After going to church, I've learned how to forgive the past. I strongly believe everyone has a guardian angel and that angel could be sitting right next to you or you'll meet them somewhere.

Forgiveness is a beautiful thing. If only everyone would see that.

---

*I* am thankful for a song like this because I think it helps people. I am a very strong person and have gone through a lot of tough times throughout the years that have made me this way. When I honestly think about it, there isn't one person I know who hasn't let me down at some point. My father left us during elementary school. My mother left me for a period of my high school years. My brother (ten years older) convinced me to perform sexual acts with him growing up. Friends have come; friends have gone. But through it all, I don't hate any of them. I have forgiven them because I can't change any of it.

---

*M*y parents separated and eventually divorced twenty-five years ago. I was very young at the time, and honestly don't even remember a time in my life when my parents were married. About five years ago, I found out it was because my dad had had an affair. And I found out that the woman he cheated with on my mom was the same woman who became my stepmom several years later. I had to accept what he did and move on. I still love my father, my mother, and my stepmom the same no matter what. My dad and stepmom's mistake—while it hurts to know it now—cannot and will not ever change the deep and unconditional love I have for them.

---

*I* cannot change that I was molested by my half-brother for years until I was a preteen. I cannot change that I was also sexually abused by a male cousin and bore his two children. I cannot change that those who should have protected me never did. I lost my innocence far too young. And I cannot change the past, when I was a child, and how life happened to me. The greatest tragedy I cannot change is that my mother didn't love me, or maybe didn't know how. Yet, I can change myself. I can change how I see life. I learned to forgive, and I decided to learn to love them all in spite of it. Forgiveness is the agent of change. And now, I care for my mother, in my home, out of love.

---

*I* was raped last March by a man I was in a relationship with. It changed my entire life. I thought that I had been damaged forever by this event, but God blessed me with people who love me and who led me to a job that I love and a man I can't live without. Through the pain of that event I found myself. I will never again be the girl I was, but I find that I like more and more every day the woman that I am. This is the first time that I have ever openly discussed it. I want to dispense the best advice I know for someone surviving rape that an amazing friend gave me: Find something you're passionate about and surround yourself in it. Then find people that you're passionate about and surround yourself with them. Repeat this until that event no longer owns you. You will heal. You'll find yourself again. This time the you that you find will be stronger, smarter, better, and happier than the you that you were. This advice is truer than anything I have ever heard. I am living proof. I am a survivor, and I am happier than ever. This song is a reminder of a time and reflection of a place that I am in now. Life is good; and take this advice if you are in a place where you need it.

---

*T*his song has been the strength of many lost and lonely nights for me! From an early age I knew I was different. Growing up my parents tried to give me the best love that they knew, but failed to show me that love and never really supported me in anything I dreamed of doing. At the age of thirteen I gave my life to the Lord, and I ended up meeting one of the most influential people in my life. She was truly an angel God sent to me. After about seven years of building a relationship with her, she moved away and disappeared out of my life. So in return

I ended up back where I started, feeling isolated and alone. I struggled to find my identity for many years. Along the way I made some terrible decisions that put me into situations where I got raped and drugged one night at a party. The emotional damage of that event brought back terrifying memories of being molested as a child. I have fought so hard for so many years to reclaim my identity, and now at the age of twenty-three I am finally seeing and accepting myself for who I am. I accept the events I cannot change, but forgive the ones I can!

---

*W*hen God was taking my aunt away from me last year this was the song that made me realize it wasn't worth hating her. I miss her and all her goodness each and every day, but I am so thankful for the forty-five years she was given here in this world. I have learned to let go of my anger for all the loved ones I've lost this year and in the past due to cancer. I've learned to forgive God for all the pain my family and others like mine have endured, and I've learned to love my family all the more.

---

*W*hen I was nine years old, I was put through something that no child should ever have to go through by a man I loved and trusted. For a while I just didn't think about it and went through life like a normal child. Around the age of fourteen, everything seemed to come out. I started withdrawing from family, school, and friends. I went into a depression and over the next four years it just got worse. Finally my mom begged me to get help. I went through a year of therapy and was finally able to stop blaming myself and just tried to move on. I became pregnant at the age of nineteen. My son is now the most wonderful thing that has ever happened to me. He's made me want to be better not only for him but for myself, too.

---

*I* had a very abusive childhood. Dad was a loving man but alcohol changed him into an abusive, raging fool. He hurt me a lot. My mother was mentally ill and beat me all day, every day. My baby sister died a few years ago. I have grown children now and some say that I overindulge them. Nevertheless, they are my heroes. I have to let go, I have to forgive, I will learn to love. Very hard, so hard to do, but I will.

---

*I*'ve had some rough times in my life. My dad cheated on my mom with a client from work and ended up marrying the client. I've hated her, and I know I have no control over my dad's actions, but I will never ever make any effort to have any kind of relationship with my stepmom. I know I should forgive my dad, but I can't. However, "What I Cannot Change" has helped me through this.

$\mathcal{W}$hen I heard "What I Cannot Change" for the first time, it brought me to tears. I grew up in a broken home and until recently had no idea who my biological father was. I have found him after thirty years and have had a lot of mixed emotions. This song I just relate to on so many levels. I have anger toward my mother for not telling me about him ... but I have to learn to let go. I am getting better with the emotions every day.

$\mathcal{I}$t seems everything I love in life has left or disappointed me. I spent five years in a Florida prison, although I've lived my life always trying to abide by the law. I was actually accused of rape by an ex-girlfriend who I would have walked through fire for. At that time I only wanted revenge in the worst way. Fortunately, time has healed those wounds and I was able to write a book about the situation and heal through that. I never thought I would be able to write and now I'm working on a couple more books. Thanks for the inspiration and to know there are other ways to deal effectively with the dark times.

*Faith*

*I* had my daughter Briley two weeks after my birthday last year. She was born premature at twenty-two weeks. It's been the hardest thing I've had to go through. My daughter weighed only one pound, one ounce and was only eleven inches long. Sometimes I feel like it's my fault. And I want to change everything. It's hard to let go and move on with life. All I have is her hospital blanket and her footprints. I never thought this would happen to me. It has taught me so much about life. We cannot control what happens to us.

———·——

*I* don't believe in coincidence, and I've always believed that if God wants to speak to us. He finds a way. For me the way was always through music. After hitting the lowest point in my life and believing that the only answer was suicide, a caring hand kept me alive and helped me to see that all the tragedies in my life were being forced to the surface for a reason. There's only so long you can hide from abuse, particularly when you lock yourself in a repetitive cycle of it. When I finally recognized where I was standing, I heard God's voice in this song. "I will learn to let go what I cannot change, but I will change whatever I can"—it's my mantra now, and there with me on the road to Heaven.

———·——

*I*n September 2008, we were at a playground celebrating my grandson's eighth birthday. My daughter and grandson's mother, Sheri, went up the slide several times with him. Her last trip down, she was in a somersault and broke her neck. God took her home at the very young age of twenty-eight. The past month has been the longest of my life. She was my very best friend. I miss her more than words can say. I know that this can't be changed in any way. Right now I am just looking for answers. There is a reason for everything, and in time I will get answers. I want to pray for anybody out there who has lost a child. It's the worst feeling in the world.

---

*T*he thing I cannot change is the murder of my twenty-five-year-old son. He's my baby, and the father of four beautiful girls who will never get to really know their daddy and the husband of a wonderful woman who is way too young to be left this way. His murder is still under investigation. It has been a year, a month, and twelve days since we lost him. I miss him so, but know I have two more girls (his older sisters), their children, and my loving, wonderful husband to live for and find life with.

I cannot change this fact in our lives, but I can love more and live more because each breath and moment we have is a blessing. You never know when you see someone if it will be your last chance to say "I love you."

*T*here are so many people without incomes and jobs now. It is frightening to think one could be homeless and living on the streets. It seems it may be happening to one member of my family, my son. He has always been responsible and does not do drugs or drink or smoke. He worked his way through college, got his degree, and then nothing. He has tried for a year and a half to get a job, any job. He helps children and old people. He made a piece of artwork that says, Make a Difference. He won't allow me to help him. He says he may have to live in his car. How many people live in their cars?

I pray to let God take care of him.

---

*I* lost my daughter in an accident in January 2006 and it tore a huge hole in my heart. It took my breath away. All the strength that I had. All I could do when I came home from the hospital was lie on her bedroom floor and cry and hold her toys. I lost a piece of my heart and soul on that terrifying and dreadful day. When I heard the song "What I Cannot Change" it made me burst into tears because it hit so close to home for me. I am still learning to let go what I cannot change. Even though my daughter is not physically here, she is here in my heart and soul, and I feel her everywhere I go. I miss her so much, but this song has put a comfort in my heart when I listen to it. I won't cry anymore, but I will always smile, because I feel blessed to have even known her for the short time she was here.

---

*T*wenty years ago, my sixteen-year-old daughter was the designated driver in a car with three very drunk twenty-one-year-old young men. When she wouldn't drive faster, one of the guys put his foot over hers on the gas pedal, and when they reached 80+ miles per hour, the car went out of control, killing my daughter and one of the men. Prior to that time, I was a singer/songwriter. It took me twenty years to start writing again. Since I began writing six months ago, it is like a dam has broken inside me. I had no idea that by letting go of the pain, I was also letting go of the creativity inside of me, making it possible for me to find once again the person I was before the accident. I have never been so happy and so fulfilled in my life as I am today. I recently signed my first contract and will be getting my first cut in Nashville for one of my songs. I am hoping that through this and through my music I can reach out now to other parents who have lost a child.

---

*I* cannot change what is in the past now that it has been nine months. I lost my big brother this year and we fought all the time, even until the day he died. I wanted to change that before he left me, but I never had the chance. I can change the way I act toward the people who are left in my life.

———

Growing up a child of an alcoholic has changed me. I suffer with control issues, trying to control anything I can because my home life was so out of control. My mother was almost always drunk, but I was very close with her regardless. She passed away in November 2007. This past year has been very difficult, trying to deal with her death and learning to let go. This song has touched my soul like no other. Learning to forgive, let go, and know there are things and people I cannot change. I am trying to live by these words, but it's hard. Learning to love again, to trust, forgive, and accept is very difficult. It makes things a little easier knowing there are others who feel the same way.

———

I have found strength and healing listening to this song. I lost my son in November when his motorcycle hit a car that ran a stop sign. He was the heart of our family and would have been twenty-seven in December. There is no relief from the grief, but this song helps me sort through all the pain and find some peace.

———

*W*hen I was thirteen years old I lost not only my best friend and hero but also my mother. Since her death it has been very tough every day for me. I am now twenty-three years old, and the feelings and memories I had are fading. I don't know if I am blocking them or just don't want to remember. I can't remember things I wish I could, like the way she smelled or the way she laughed. Throughout my life I always wanted to do something that matters to myself and other people. But no matter what I do, it seems to be wrong. I have become obese, which sucks because I am having a hard time finding a man who loves me. One day I hope to try to overcome these feelings and love myself for me and no one else.

---

*I*'ve lived through the tragedy of losing a fiancé in a car accident, my father two days later to suicide, and many other challenges and struggles, but I still always seem to feel the pain of others and wish I could take it away. My heart goes out to LeAnn and all her fans who connect to this song on deep levels due to their own personal journeys through life. How wonderful to be able to touch so many people in so many different ways. For me today the song makes me want to move, it lifts my spirit, it motivates me, it makes me appreciate where I am and what I have, and that is an amazing thing to happen from just listening to a song.

---

*M*y child died. My husband died. Telling me I need to mourn doesn't tell me how to mourn. If I talk about it, then I just want attention. If I suppress it, then I'm cold. I want to be liked. I need to be loved. Will I ever be loved like that again? I bottle my emotions and plant them in the pit of my stomach. People who annoy me aren't bad people. A sane person would smile and nod and politely excuse themselves. Not me. I cut them down at the knees because I'm having a bad day . . . week . . . year. I cannot change the fact that people die before their time. I cannot change the fact that my heart will never be whole again.

I will learn to let go of some of the pain.

I will learn to forgive . . . everyone.

I will learn to love myself . . . mankind . . . God . . . and life.

But mostly I will just learn, because if you don't live to learn then there really isn't any point in living at all.

———

*L*ast June my son took his life. He served our country. Because of my drug use, I lost custody of him twenty years ago. I tried and didn't make it back into his life. Now he is forever gone from my arms. I tired to mend the hurt and ask for forgiveness over the years. He wasn't ready for that to happen. I heard about his death in an e-mail from a family member. I've been clean for some years now, but my family still holds me at bay. The angels hold my son and heal his hurts. I hope he rests in peace and knows that I've always loved him.

*T*his song has always torn at my emotions. My husband of eighteen years passed away from cancer when I was fifty-one and he was fifty-five. That was six years ago. I still face dark days but I find great comfort in a little angel by the name of Connie, who is there to listen to me. I don't want pity from anyone, because that emotion only tends to drag me down and prevents me from moving forward. It really hurts to read other people's stories and see that my grief is pale compared to others' anguish in life. Certain songs still tug at my heart, but instead of denying myself this human emotion, I now sit down and listen intently to the words and reflect back to things we shared. Relying on the Creator and family has also helped. In 2006 my daughter blessed me with a beautiful granddaughter. This delightful bundle of joy was given to me as a replacement for what I lost six years ago. I pray every night that my children have me to comfort them, too. Never take something for granted, because it can be gone in a second.

*M*y father and I had a strained relationship. I am now fifty-four years old. My dad passed away four years ago. The last words I spoke to him in the hospital were "I love you, Dad." Those words were very seldom spoken between the two of us. I visited my father's grave a few weeks after his passing. I talked to my dad that afternoon in a way I wish I had when he was still alive. I told him he was a good man and a good father. When I left his grave, I stopped at a playground in my old neighborhood and sat in the very swings I used to play on as a child. When I stood up to leave, the merry-go-round behind me was spinning very fast. I was alone there on the playground. No one else was there. I know my father heard me.

---

*I*n August I said good-bye to my daughter Cathy. She was an asthmatic and had an attack that put her into a coma from which she never recovered. She had three children, who are seventeen, fourteen, and six. I cannot change what happened the day of her attack, yet I am constantly asking the what-ifs. God did bless me with her last year of life, as we moved in together for financial reasons. I watched her get out of a bad relationship and move into the most important relationship of her life. She truly fell in love and told me a week before she died, "Mom, for the first time in my life I know I am truly loved." I thank God for this. With the grace of God time will heal, but we shall miss her so as she was our laughter and joy.

---

*M*y father and I were close, but got even closer as the years moved on. My father died in September 2005. I miss him dearly and I often think of him when I see my adult son. I think I see my father's style in my son's ways. I still have my father's ashes. I plan to scatter them in a wonderful natural spring in Florida, my favorite place in the whole world. He liked it, too. Dad, you would be proud of your grandson.

---

*I* cannot change my grandma's death. She died of lung and brain cancer. I miss her so much, and I think about her every day. I think of all the memories I had with her. She was a great cook. She made banana bread, potato salad, brownies—almost anything she cooked came out great. The day before her death I went to her house, and I felt bad because I was very close to saying, Oh, I'll go tomorrow, but I'm glad I went. That night I knelt at the side of my bed, and I prayed for her. . . . I was about to cry when I saw her; she lay there still, without talking, and taking very abnormal breaths. Now, I really miss her a lot. I was very close to her.

---

*I* cannot change that my dad died of bone cancer in 2005. I miss him every day and pray that he is at peace. I am an oncology nurse, and even though I save people every day, I could not save my dad. I have so much guilt in my heart because I feel like I let him down. I know it sounds silly for me to feel this way, but I still do. My dad is my hero, and he is the reason I do what I do. I talk with him daily and yearn to hear his deep Southern voice. I know I will never be able to enjoy him or hear him laugh again, and it absolutely kills me. I know that I cannot change his death, but I wish I could every day, and I probably always will.

---

*I* have learned that what I cannot change is the fact that my boyfriend died at the age of twenty-eight from cancer. I have learned that I will never see him again, we will not get married, or have children or ever get to kiss one another again. I have learned that at some point I am going to have to let go of him, and myself, if I ever want to find love again.

---

*T* oday at 11:00 A.M. I lost the most important man in my life. He was my grandfather. My best friend. I was his princess, and as he called me from day one, his golden girl. It's so hard. I came out to Colorado to help him not knowing his time was soon. I did what I could. And everyone saw a change in him immediately. He would always smile when I came into the room. I feel so lost and numb. I don't know what to do. I want to help with something, but everyone is telling me there's nothing for me to do. He was an amazing man. He died from pneumonia. Now I'm writing a cookbook of his favorite recipes in his honor.

*I* have two beautiful little girls. Last June they lost their dad to a motorcycle accident. Their dad and I were married for almost ten years when his accident happened. There is so much about our relationship that I wish I could change, but the only thing I can do now is to learn from my mistakes and try to make things better in the next relationship that I have. Every day I live with looking in my little girls' eyes and seeing the empty space where their dad once was. What I cannot change is the fact that their dad is gone, but I can be there for them every day for the rest of their lives.

*I* have had a hard life. My mother was my best friend, but she sadly died in 1998 from cancer. It was a hard time for my family and me indeed. My dad has been engaged twice, once to a coworker at his job and now to a family friend. Granted I love my future step-mom, but for years I have hated my dad for marrying her. I still miss my mother. I guess I just have taken her death out on my dad for no reason. He is one person in my life that I can't change. He has the right to be happy now.

*T*wo and a half years ago I was torn apart by a friend whose child might die without a liver transplant. About a month after meeting her, my world changed again. I was called to my dad's side. He died just as my mom and I got to his side. As I was faced with losing my dad, I was thinking of the little girl who needed the liver. Nothing could be done for my dad; I only hoped that the little girl would not leave me next. I had grown attached quickly. A few months later the little girl went in for a transplant. I feel God sent her to help me get past what I could not change. She survived and is great.

---

*W*ithin this year I lost my three best friends and first love to the ways of the world: lying, betrayal, sex, and drugs. One of these best friends was my alcoholic mother. There were times when I would turn all the lights off in my room and just cry in solitude and darkness, not knowing when I would be able to turn the lights on again. Everyone I had ever trusted or loved seemed to have turned their back on me. Singing was my escape from my turbulent home life and social circle. When I turned on "What I Cannot Change" in my dark room one evening, the light came back. I realized that I could love what I couldn't change.

---

*T*his song has brought me to tears for many reasons. In life, through trials and mistakes, I have learned that I am not in control. The times I tried to control my life, I realized that God is in control. There are things we cannot change. People we can choose to forgive, even though they don't change. Things we can let go of. My mom has cancer. It's been a fight for three and a half years. It took two years for me to accept. Once we let go and forgive what we cannot change, we are set free. This song hits home to me. I was mad at cancer. I hated God. I blamed God. But then I realized in this life if you don't feel pain or disappointment, you don't appreciate it.

---

*I* cannot change that I decided to have an abortion. Although it was five years ago, I still am not 100 percent sure it was the correct thing to do. I am a busy, successful person and have a decent life. And I have a two-year-old son. The overwhelming joy, love, and appreciation he has brought to my life still makes me upset at myself that I didn't have the courage to have my first baby five years ago. I hate what I did and don't think I thought it through hard enough before acting. I still punish myself subconsciously, and I know I need to make peace with the decision. It is definitely something that I cannot change. But I will learn to let go . . . someday, perhaps.

---

*I*t was five years yesterday that my husband drowned trying to save a boy who had been pulled out into the ocean by a riptide.

The boy was okay, but my husband did not make it. I have learned to let go of the anger. I have learned to forgive my husband for leaving me. I am now married again to a wonderful man and we have a son. I strive every day to learn to love freely without the fear of losing.

---

*M*y marriage broke up in 2002. I moved two thousand miles back West and worked three jobs nearly nonstop to get settled. I realized I was not only down from the separation, but that I could not stand myself anymore. What I finally found out was that I needed to remind myself what went right each day. I wrote down what went right versus what went wrong in my day. The sun was up. Breakfast tasted good. After doing this every day, I realized I allowed ten minutes of stress to ruin twenty-three hours and fifty minutes. Since then I thank God for what I have. I have found fantastic friends, a new job, and a song that helped me heal.

*Family and Friends*

*I* have a sister who is really struggling for a job right now, and I really miss her. My parents ask if I want her back, and I must lie or they will get mad. My parents are always fighting, and we never get to spend time with them. It seems like they don't think we are good kids. I am a teen, and they think we are always up to something. I have another sister, who is having a really tough time. She and I are like best friends. I am home-schooled and I don't get out much. I have a job at a senior citizen center, and we have to clean every Wednesday. If something is wrong our mom yells at us, saying we need to do better. It's like we aren't good enough for them. I am an Eastern Orthodox Christian, and I don't get to go to church much, so that is hard. I am trying to keep it together, but it is so hard. I am so close to breaking. My parents have threatened to divorce, and it scares me so much. I am only fifteen, and it is so hard. I tried to tell my mom something about her late husband, and she wouldn't believe me. I hate it. I have just said what I have been holding in for five years.

---

*I* love the song. It made me realize that I can't change people. Everyone makes choices in life and you can't make someone do something just because it's right. They have to live with their decisions. I have had an off-and-on relationship with my dad for the last twenty-five years. He married a woman who doesn't accept that there was life before her. She does everything she can to make sure my dad doesn't see his only grandson and me. I have blamed her for many years, but have come to realize in the last several years that he is just as much to blame. He allowed this to happen. He allowed her to force his hand and decide between his only daughter and her. Unfortunately, he chose her. I have struggled with this for many years, and after hearing this song, it made me realize that it's not healthy for me to harbor this hatred. I should just let it go. I can't change either of them. I need to focus on my family, my husband, and my son. Hopefully someday my dad will realize what he's done and come to me. But in the meantime, I've got to live my own life and accept that it's probably not going to include him. And that's his loss, not mine.

---

*N*othing hurts more than knowing that no matter how much you love a person, even more than yourself, they will never love you back the same way. I have been married for a while now, but I have struggled so much because I do not know where I stand. Every day I wake up with feelings of uncertainty, not knowing if this could be the day that I have been dreading.

---

$\mathcal{W}$hen I was in high school my mother abandoned my brothers and me, and we were forced to live in the most difficult circumstances. I was so dedicated my senior year, but I didn't get as far as I wished I would have because my mother left us. Eventually, I became stronger and overcame this bump in the road. Like many others I have learned to live life for me and not for others. And to think I almost took my own life because my mother wasn't listening to my yearning and callings for help.

---

$\mathcal{I}$ knew that I was very different from an early age. It wasn't until I was a teenager that I realized that I was gay. It was hard growing up gay in a conservative family in the South. Because of LeAnn and her music I am still here. I am still alive, and I am okay. There is nothing wrong with me. I will learn to let go of what I cannot change.

---

$\mathcal{I}$ come from a divorced family. I am the oldest of five siblings who all live in three separate homes within thirty miles of one another. All my life I have taken the responsibility of being the pseudo-parent, putting myself last. I have struggled to be a perfect example for my younger siblings and to motivate them to do the best they possibly can. I also try my best to help my parents as much as possible because I know how hard it can be. It gets hard trying to balance school, work, and helping with family. I listen to this song whenever I am having a moment of weakness. It helps me realize that I am not perfect and that it is okay not to be. I am the best person I can be and cannot change elements that are not in my grasp.

---

This song has helped a gay man. I hope it helps his sister to understand.

---

I could write a book. I have been molested by my father and once by my uncle. I grew up in an emotionally and physically abusive home by both parents. My memories of my childhood are not happy ones, but rather painful. I have done exactly the opposite in raising my four children. They know they are loved every day regardless of any mistakes they may make along life's highway. They know I will never turn my back on them. This is my second marriage, and I thought it was one that would last forever. I learned two years ago my husband had been having an affair for more than six months. With his job, there was no way I would ever know. I decided to stay and God only knows why, because I've always said I would leave the person who cheats on me. Things are not perfect, and we still struggle. However, we are trying. Marriage is work. I have to learn to let go of the past, which is very hard. I am a forgiving person. I have learned to pray for those who hurt me and/or my family. I need to learn to love myself more. Every night I pray and thank God for all He has given me. I want to help everyone I can and let them know someone cares. Faith in God is what keeps me going through all my difficult times.

---

*I* just moved more than a thousand miles away from home to go to school. I have very little confidence in myself. Even though this has been in the works for more than a year, I'm still doubting myself. My parents and I have had a lot of arguments over the year about it because it's expensive, but it's what I want to do. It was really hard for me and my dad. We've always been close. I'm a total Daddy's girl, but there have been many, many times where we'd go for weeks and even a couple months without talking. We started to patch things up a couple months ago. This morning when I headed out, my father hugged me and said he was proud of me. I don't think he's ever said that to me.

---

*I* cannot change my anger. I cannot change the things that I hide from people on a day-to-day basis. I cannot change that for years on end, my parents hated each other. When my brother went to prison, I was sexually molested by someone I trusted, and I can't change the fact that my father recently passed away. I can change me, though. I can get help, I can talk to someone, I can make that happen. But I'm scared to because then I'll have to truly deal with all of these issues. I'm scared to get married; I'm scared that I'm not good enough to be married. Hopefully I can change and become a good person to everyone I love in my life. I won't allow my issues to stop or interrupt that.

---

*W*hat I cannot change is my father's treatment of our family. I don't ever remember him telling me or my two brothers that he loved us. The simplest dream of having a baseball catch in the backyard or doing some father/son activities was always met with negativity. Whatever we did, especially me being the oldest, was never good enough. When my parents got a divorce when I was a teenager, he pretty much disowned my mom and me. I never really felt I had a father figure. Now, as an adult with a wife and two kids of my own, hopefully I've learned what it means to show your family the love and respect that I never received.

---

*I* have survived child molestation.
I have survived domestic violence.
I have broken the chain.
I have learned to change what I thought I could not change.
I have changed.
I know what makes me tick.

I now love me.

The rest is out of my hands.

This is a heart song. Coming from your heart, going out to those who need help and to those of us who have found the ability to let go of what we cannot change and conquer what we can.

---

*I* come from a broken home. As a teenager and young adult I became sexually active—so much so that I didn't always remember their names the next day. Sometimes it was two different men in the same night. Now I am married with children and have always been faithful. I love my husband, but I can't change the fact that I shared a part of myself with those men and cannot take it back. I wish so much that I didn't have that past, but I can't change it. I can change who I am today and grow from who I was in the past. I am a good mother and wife, and I am learning to let go of what I cannot change.

---

*I* am a twenty-six-year-old wife and mother of four. I have been married for seven years this last August and my oldest child is six. I sometimes feel myself regretting jumping into a marriage and having children. Even though I would not change anything with my children. I love them to death, I just feel held back now. I am trying to go to college and become a wildlife ecologist, but it is hard when you have a family and a husband to fit in, too. I can relate to this song because I come from a very dysfunctional family. My mother and father used my brother and me as pawns in their divorce, which caused a great deal of pain. I have grown up hoping to avoid the same direction my parents went, but I am so worried that I will be the next to follow. So I grasp onto my marriage so tight that I am starting to realize maybe I don't need to.

I need to do what the song says, learn to let go, forgive, and love.

---

*J*am a twenty-year-old man. During my childhood, I suffered a lot. I am an only child. My mom was so overprotective. I remember I used to feel alone, and I was afraid of everything. People at school, my classmates, used to laugh at me, saying things like "$#@!" My mom never really understood the fact that I was different. She tried, against my own will, to make me behave the way she wanted. I was five or seven years old when I started feeling guilty and sad because no one could understand that I was not like everybody else. During my teen years, I finally could admit to myself that I was feeling sexually interested in other boys. But it wasn't easy. My relationship with my father became very difficult. I had bad times at home and at school. I would cry a lot, and even hurt myself. I gained weight as a result of my emotional issues. Now I'm struggling to lose weight. I have dreams.

I want to be a psychologist. I want to learn how to play a guitar. I want to sing because I love it. Sometimes the past comes to haunt me. Some memories are hard to deal with, but I'll never give up. I have to fight against my compulsive eating. But I know for sure I'll be free one day.

———

*I* can totally understand the words "it's easier to please the world than please myself." I too feel that way: some days it's easier to please everyone else than do what makes me happy. I wish so many times that I could turn back time and change the things I have done, but listening to this song I realize I cannot change these times. Instead I can forgive and learn to love what I have.

# Depression

*I* cannot change the fact that I feel so alone in this world. Everyone who has ever been important to me has turned their back and walked out of my life. I don't understand why I'm not good enough for someone to love. Every day I question what is wrong with me and why I'm not good enough. I feel I have the biggest heart and so much to offer but no one wants me in return. I give and give and give but never get anything back. I pray someday someone will see the good in me and the love I have to offer.

---

*M* y life the past two weeks has been difficult and frustrating, as each and every day gets worse. I just graduated college and am struggling to find work. My parents don't believe in my dreams or me. I can't get a girlfriend, and I have low self-esteem. I was ready to give up on this life but this song made me light up in a way I haven't felt before. Suddenly things weren't so bad because no matter who doesn't believe in me, I believe in myself.

---

*S* omewhere in Long Beach, California, sat a forty-year-old woman in her car crying her soul clean and all because of the way a song had touched her. It was seven years and four months after being told that I would be living the rest of my life with what they call bipolar disorder. They say that healing often sneaks up on you, and I was being flooded with memories and feelings—I cried, and I cried hard. I thought of all the things that I have lost and what will never be, yet I celebrate each day. I have to let go and change what I am able to change and make a difference in someone's life. My daughter, who is fourteen, also has bipolar disorder, and she heard this song in the car on the CD and said, "Mom, that was so great, it was like she was singing to you." I looked at her with tears and said, "No, baby, she is singing to us."

---

*I* heard this song for the first time this morning on my way into work. So many thoughts went through my head. Yes, I believe that everyone has something they believe they cannot change, but there may be a corner they haven't searched, a rock they haven't turned over. I believe a person's happiness is truly up to them because no one can change that for them. I've been through depression, and my boyfriend suffers from depression. Sometimes I want to shake some sense into him, but we deal with what we can together—the rest is up to him. We're both overweight, we both drink too much, but I can change only my end of it. I am a pretty happy person, and that makes a huge difference. I'm not looking up at the world from some deep well, but I'll be there to help my friends out if they ask. Heartache happens to everyone—it's what makes us human.

*I* know that we all have our good days and bad days, but sometimes I wish that the bad days would stay far away from me. I am a twenty-eight-year-old wife and mother of four boys. My life has been turned upside down since I lost my second son in 2002. He was only six months old. I blame myself for his death due to the fact that I had left the bathroom for only a second and he drowned in a bathtub in our home. I now live in a different state and have no family or friends but my husband's. Since my son's death I have had two more children who I love very much. It's been hard to see them and wonder what my son would look like if he were still alive. A parent should never have to bury their children. I would have never guessed that my life would turn out this way. The music helps us understand that it's okay to feel the way we feel and that there are other people out there who are just like you and me. I hope you can understand that music is a way for us to cry, laugh, and dance.

*I* have suffered with depression, low self-esteem, and suicidal thoughts since I started high school. Sometimes the pain I was feeling brought me so low that in a breakdown of tears, I'd cut myself. It is an ongoing process, and I struggle with feeling better about my life and myself every day, but hearing your music and the struggles you face and attempt to deal with every day gives me hope and tells me that I should do the same.

I will learn to let go of my low self-esteem and internalizing emotions about the hurtful things people have said to me. On most occasions, the people who said hurtful things to me said them to me simply because I was there. They would have said the same thing regardless of who was there at the time.

I will learn to forgive those who have hurt me. I need to come up with ways to think about the things people say to me to help me not to internalize their harsh words.

I will learn to love that I'm a beautiful, intelligent, worldly girl with a great sense of humor and a naturally athletic build. I do not need to hurt myself because I am feeling low. There are better ways to handle it.

---

*M*y heart is heavy with sadness and I cry in silence every day. There are numerous genuine causes for my despondency, and I try each day to accept the things I cannot change. My grandmother had a favorite prayer that I find myself saying each day. When I heard this song it touched me—as this is my prayer. I hope it will help anyone who has not yet heard it. God grant me the serenity to accept the things I cannot change, the courage to change the things I can, and the wisdom to know the difference.

*I* had a very difficult childhood. I am forty-six years old and still find myself haunted by the past. I suffer from depression that some days are so dark that I often think that suicide is the answer. I have no one to talk to because I do not trust them. I cannot love anyone because my heart has been broken too many times. It is so empty and it hurts. I often feel that my life would be better off if I were not here anymore. I have listened to this song so many times and just cannot seem to quit crying. I think to myself that only I can change my life, but where and how do you begin to repair the damage that seems to not want to go away?

I want to live.

*I* heard this song when my husband downloaded it from iTunes. At the time my husband was suffering from depression, but he was hiding it from me. I was pregnant and going through a very bad pregnancy, so I was in and out of the hospital a lot. My husband was my mountain. We had a beautiful baby boy, and we are both very healthy now. It wasn't until a year later that I found out about my husband's depression. I had no idea. We went through a very tough and soul-searching period. It tested our marriage and friendship to the limit. I had to let go of what happened and deal with what I could, as I now needed to be his rock. It is now eight months later and life is good. We take each day as it comes; we love each other with renewed passion, respect, and honesty. This song means so much to me now that I understand it perfectly.

---

*I* really don't know how to accept my life. I was unwanted, a mistake from birth. My mother was mentally unstable and abusive. I lived through physical, sexual, and psychological abuse as well as severe neglect. I've gone through life feeling as though I'm never good enough, smart enough, pretty enough, thin enough, etc. I spent much of my childhood in and out of the foster care system. I have suffered with depression, anxiety, and an eating disorder for most of my life; collateral damage, I guess. All I've ever wanted was to matter, to fit in, and to be loved. I'm still working on trying to cope with all of my issues. I've had more than my share of hard knocks, but I've finally found someone who I love deeply and would like to spend the rest of my life with. For once in my life I'm not an object or a possession, I'm a real person who is treated with love and respect. Maybe someday I'll finally be free of the lifelong prison of guilt, pain, and shame that abuse has created for me. I'd truly love to be able to forgive and love without fear, reservation, and shame. I realize that nobody can ever change what I've lived through, but I hope to live with love and forgiveness.

# Life

My husband leaves on deployment to Iraq very soon—just in time to not have him here for the holidays. I worry about him every single minute of every day. I have come to realize and accept that I am not in control of what happens to him and the men he is with. I can't change what will happen to him when he gets there. I can only love him and support him and his men.

---

I am a pre-op transsexual woman. This song of yours really spoke to me about the hardships I have gone through and am going through with my parents and family over my choice to transition and be myself. I can change myself but I cannot change them. I need to accept that. Thank you so much for the inspiration. Now I pray for the strength.

---

What I cannot change is that I had an abortion. Every single day I live with that regret.

---

I cannot change the fact that my brother is a drug addict, but I do love him. I wish I could change that for him, but he has to do it himself. I feel like the things I'm struggling with in my life are small potatoes compared to others and do not warrant the same kind of reaction. I have always wished for a magic wand to make everything in the world right again. Maybe one day it will come.

---

*I* cannot change that I fail a little bit every day, some more than others. And that I still dwell on one mistake I made two years ago that someone else can't forgive me for.

---

*I*'ve never met my real father since he left my mom and me. I wonder about him every day. My mom remarried when I was seven, but we've never had much of a relationship. All my life I've felt like something was missing or that I wasn't good enough. I really don't talk about my feelings much, or have anyone I can talk to about it. I know I cannot change what has happened. I just hope that I can let go of the pain I feel every day because of this. I'm not sure if I'll ever want to meet him or have the guts to go see him. The fact is, he's had twenty years to come see me or call and he never has. And he only lives about twenty miles away.

---

*I* am a thirty-year-old married mom of two. My mom died when I was two from cancer, and I have no memory of her. My father never talked about my real mom and really never tried to be close to me. I left home at sixteen because I just couldn't deal with my stepmom anymore. I have two younger brothers who I hated to leave behind, but at sixteen, I didn't realize the effects of my decision. I try to this day to be close to them, but they are distant in many ways. Six months after leaving home I was attacked and raped in the middle of the night. It was so terrifying. The man came back into our home five different times, raping my grandmother at one point as well. I was never the same. I moved away with my boyfriend and he helped me through the worst time of my life. We have been together for fourteen years now and have two boys. Since my ordeal, I lost my beloved grandmother, a cousin to a drunk driver, an uncle to a shooting, and all my possessions in a house fire. I am a shy, untrusting individual now and wish I could be more social for my husband's and kids' sakes. I carry feelings of anger, guilt, sadness, envy, and fear, all for things I cannot change. I am forever changed by my past but am still strong in my faith somehow.

---

*W*e cannot change everything that we would like to, but we should learn to forgive and love those around us, including ourselves, and to change what we can. Like changing our views on life, love, and happiness. The world is full of things right now that truly need to be changed, but we can't do it alone, and it can't be done overnight. We must accept these things for what they are and try to live a better life so that change will one day take place, and we will all be better for it.

---

*I* married a man who I thought I was in love with, and now we have two children who are the light of my life. I feel so blessed, but my husband continues to break my heart, and I want a life of my own. I am not strong enough to leave him nor do I have the funds to do so. I stay in the marriage because I cannot change who he is, so I just pray and hope that God will change my heart and the situation for the better. I miss who I was before, but I would never give up one day without my children. I love them so much. I just wish my husband would realize what he has.

---

*I* am a gay man and had a hard time accepting and living with my sexuality for many, many years. I was a drug addict for years as well. . . . Hiding from others and myself. I came out eleven years ago and met my life partner and soul mate eight years ago. I have never been happier. Today I say a thank-you prayer every day to God, Mother Nature, and my universe for all the gifts I have been blessed with. Although it has taken me years to get here, I would not change a thing about the journey. It has made me who I am today: happy, whole, thankful, loved, and confident. I connect so well to the lyrics of the song. If we could all only let go of what we cannot change, we would all be a lot happier and content with the life we are living. All we can do is try to make good choices, live, love, laugh, and learn.

---

*I* have an idyllic life—an amazing husband and between us, five beautiful, healthy children. I find myself letting the stresses of everyday life cloud the beauty around me. I would be devastated to lose anyone in my life. Hearing this song brought me to a place of quiet within myself to let go of those things I can't change and be thankful for what's around me right here, right now.

I'm so blessed, and I want to be able to share what I have, to develop lasting relationships with my children, and teach them what really matters in life.

---

*F*inding someone who understands me seems like finding a needle in a haystack. A good day will overtake me and leave me with memories to pass over all of the dark, gloomy ones that seem to whittle away. My past is like a giant magnet that keeps pulling me back because I can't seem to get it out of my head. Every day something or someone will remind me of when my stepdad cornered me. How dutiful I was for nine long years to service him in the way he saw fit. To protect my sister and earn my keep I also endured verbal and sometimes physical abuse. All the while, my mom was in love with him, working or going back to school, and was caught up in his bar life, drinking and doing what he wanted. Today I am twenty, and living only with what I was taught. I'm struggling to find God's way and the right path for my life. Ignoring what had happened in the past, I am now just coming to terms with it. And it was real. This song speaks to me. I need to follow my heart, and my heart is singing.

*Sobriety*

*I* cannot change an addict. They have the right to drink and drug themselves into the grave, and I have the right not to follow them there. We can only change ourselves and not those around us. The only option is to leave an addict, not change them. I left my alcoholic girlfriend almost a year ago. I thought she was the love of my life, but she wasn't. I can't change her, she has to change herself, and I pray for her sake she does.

---

*I* will learn to let go of the fact that my brother is killing himself and destroying his family using drugs. I have tried to help him, but there is nothing I can do if he won't help himself. It's strange because it's almost as if he's already dead to me. I'm sure he will be soon if he continues down this road.

---

*T*his song got me through a lot of really hard times. I'm only thirteen but have gone through a lot in my short lifetime. My grandma that I basically grew up with was a very heavy alcoholic. She would get drunk and just start hitting me. She never hurt my older brother—just me. I beat myself up for the longest time wondering what I did that made her hate me so bad to abuse me. Now I realize she couldn't help it—she was just very sick. Then when I was nine my parents went through a horrible divorce. We found out just a few months after the divorce that my dad was engaged and had a kid and another on the way with his fiancée. All that took a real long time to get used to, but I'm so thankful now that I did. I wouldn't trade my family for anything. I think "What I Cannot Change" is the best song ever. I'm so glad I found a song I can listen to to help me through my dark times.

———

*I* have had a rough life. My mother was married eleven times. I started at a young age thinking I knew what life was. I met my son's father at sixteen, had my first child at eighteen. I was in a very abusive relationship for ten years. He held knives to my throat and guns to my head numerous times. I had black eyes, but I swore never to get divorced. I thought I could make it work. Well, I found out the hard way I can't change him. I then started using drugs and went straight to the top as I thought. I lived that crazy life for a while then tried to leave. Needless to say, I moved to a different state to leave. I then met my second child's father. I started to be a dancer. My God, where the hell did my life go? Things just kept going on and on and on. Then I tried sobriety. The best thing that has happened in my life. Now I have three beautiful children and am trying to go back to school to work an honest, reliable job so I can live in a home for my children and me. Those things that happened in my life I cannot change, but I can do something for today and that is to be clean, sober, and honest.

---

*I* am a recovering meth addict. I've been clean for six years now with no want or desire to ever be trapped in that dark place ever again. It took all I had and all I was just to make it from day to day. I woke up one morning and realized what I had done to myself and more so to those who had cared about me. My problem wasn't just mine, it was everyone's around me as well. I never saw that until it was too late. Now my life is very full and I am in a very happy place. Each day I wake up, it is a new beginning; and although I can't change the past, the future is out there calling my name. And even though I realize it was easy for me to overcome, it's not for others. I just want to say: Believe and accept the things you cannot change, grow with them, and change the things you can and always believe that you are worth it. Do not worry about what others think; your opinion of yourself is the one that matters the most. I am a forty-six-year-old man who embraces life every day looking back at those seventeen years of addiction only long enough to remind myself of the beautiful future to come.

---

*I* wish I could change my son's life. His father got him into drugs twelve years ago. And it hurts me really bad to see him like that. But I know he has to help himself, I can't change him. I love him with my whole heart.

———·———

*My* husband is a recovering drug addict and has been sober for fifteen years. I can learn to accept and forgive the understanding and struggles my husband has to go through when this disease robs him of his spiritual essence daily. A girlfriend and I started a women's support group for women to vent about pretty much anything, instead of taking it out on our children or other loved ones. When I was struggling with my understanding of addiction, I wrote in my journal—but with the support and faith of my husband, I made it into a book for others to realize that they are not alone in this world with those outlandish thoughts of regret, unfaithfulness, anger, and especially fear.

———·———

*I* have had the worst two years of my life. My kids were taken by cops when they were two and a half and five weeks. We got them back after seven months. Well, you see, I am a recovering alcoholic. Four months sober. My husband got domestic on me in July 2008 in front of the kids. He had custody. I could not live at home due to my addictions. So I left him for good. And the kids were taken again. What I'm saying here is thank you for this song. I needed it.

*I* grew up in a home surrounded by drugs and emotional abuse. In school, I was the fat, awkward girl who stood alone off in the corner just trying to get through the day avoiding as many stares as possible. I usually came home crying, and—more often than not—considered suicide. All I've ever wanted in my life is to be a wife and a mother, to have a family of my own. I'm twenty-seven years old and have never had a serious relationship, and in fact I am only starting to gain a relationship with myself where I actually like me—and I'm finally starting to build my life rather than waiting for it to happen. For the first time in my life, I'm happy and patiently waiting on God's promise.

*W*hen I was a child my mom always had lots of parties. That's when I picked up my first drink of coffee brandy. I never knew my father, but I think I might have been a different girl if he had been around—not hanging out with the wrong crowds and going to parties thinking I was cool when I really wasn't. I didn't know all that back then. Today I am a thirty-three-year-old single mom of three beautiful children who keep me sober.

My man is in a sober house now. We have been through the mud and back. Things used to get so ugly between us when he drank, and I was a bad drunk myself. Nothing good ever comes from drinking. We always say to one another, as they say in AA, one day at a time, that's all any of us can do. It's hard to stop drinking when I have done it for so long. It's like the bottle is my only friend. That is how I used to feel until I met a lot of great people from AA who are truly there for me.

# Growth

*W*hat I cannot change. I cannot change how others look at me or what they choose to believe about me. I cannot change how my heart initially reacts to others' pain or the pain that is inflicted on me. I cannot change the abuse occurring in our world in so many ways. I cannot change that I will never be a model or a genius or anything remarkable. I cannot change that one day I will lose my father and my mother and have to depend on just me to get by. But I can change how I treat myself. I can change how I treat others. I can change how I choose to view the world when I get up in the morning. Thank you for reminding me of this.

*I*'m twenty years old, and when I was sixteen I was raped. For a while I blamed myself. I consumed myself with the pain and began getting into drugs and not respecting myself. I was about eighteen when I started to have confidence and see that I am beautiful. I'm clean from drugs and I'm strong. I became a survivor because of what I can't change. I can't take what he did away, but that's fine because I can forgive, but not forget, not regret, move on, and grow. And I have. I love who I am and I have the strength to move on and one day help someone else. This song helped me open up about the one thing I cannot change.

*I* need to let go not of what others have done to me, but of what I have done to myself. It is in the past, and yet I can't seem to get past the shame of it. I constantly worry about what others are thinking, and I carry it with me wherever I go. Today I want to start moving past it and realize that life goes on. When I heard "What I Cannot Change," it mirrored my hopes for how I could view my situation and myself. I can no longer change it, it is done. But I can change the way I look at it, and I can keep it from ruining the rest of my life.

———

*I* have been through hard times since I was three years old. I've dealt with a lot. I've been out of the closet since I was thirteen. Now at twenty-one I've come to accept two mottos that I can say this song helps me live by: "Do not judge lest ye be judged" and "Each to their own." You can't change everyone, everyone has their own personality, likes, and dislikes, and who are we to judge them for that? We are all human, and we make mistakes.

———

*I* can't change the fact that I have a broken heart from the love of my life, and lost him because I am transgendered. I cannot change the fact that my mother committed suicide when I was thirteen. I cannot change the fact that I have HIV. I cannot change that I will need $18,500 for my surgery next summer.

I can change by letting go of the man I love to find his true happiness. I can remember my mother as a beautiful soul who really did love me. I can be happy that having had HIV for fifteen years, I am still healthy. I can change the fact that though I live below the poverty line, I will have the good credit to have my surgery done.

I changed and became self-employed.

---

*E*veryone has their demons, and it is how you choose to deal with them that makes us stronger. I learned a long time ago that I am who I am, and the demons in my past helped to make me the strong, beautiful, caring, loving, talented woman I am today. I thank you for your grace and beauty and the thought of expression in your song. I know that it came from a hard place, one that breaks the heart, reaches out to help, and crushes the soul when it is turned away. What I cannot change is everything, but what I want to change is nothing. I am me.

---

*M*y father and I did not talk for ten years. During that time I served with the U.S. Army as a paratrooper and was in harm's way, so to speak. It wasn't until after my wife pushed me to talk to him that I found we are so very much alike. Now we have at last become friends. Family is priceless (even with all the warts) and can never be replaced when gone. Make peace with them while they are here for when our time comes, it comes.

---

*I* can't change my parents' personality disorders or how those impacted us as children. I can change who I choose to have in my life. I have a right to be treated with dignity and respect and a right to say no.

---

*I* know in my life I have made a lot of mistakes, and sometimes I feel like those mistakes haven't developed into a resolution. I lost my brother when he was six, and even though I know it was not my fault, I still feel like I could have done something to alter the worst. After he passed, things got worse with my family. I would like to let go what I cannot change. I cannot change the fact that my brother is not here anymore, but I have learned a lot and have realized that I have to forgive myself and realize that there are people out there who I still have to live for.

---

*T*he very day I heard this song it had been one of the worst days of my life. My father was never really in my life, only when it was convenient for him to be. It was very hard for me growing up without a dad in my life, even though I would never have admitted it back then. I tried to be the strong one and hold my feelings in for my mom and my mentally handicapped brother. Well, the day I heard this song, I found out that he had said some very hurtful things about me that I just couldn't even fathom a parent saying about his child. I had so many feelings at that time that all I did was cry and lean on my loved ones. And then I heard this song, and it was like someone hit the switch (*you* hit the switch). It was then that I realized no matter how hard you try, there are going to be things you can't change, so move on from them and be happy with what you do have. In my case that was my family and friends, who have been there for me through whatever. I realized I hadn't been alone all along.

---

*I* have been divorced for seven years now, and my ex-husband remarried four years ago. He is not a part of his girls' lives anymore. He does not even call them. I struggle with that daily, as I know that they really love their dad, and being girls, they really need him to be a part of that. That is what I cannot change, so I try to be there for my girls, as their mother and their father. I can only support them, love them, and hope one day he will be there for them. When I heard this song it helped me to realize something I have to accept and then move on and do the best I can.

When I first heard this song I knew that it explained me. I am always so busy trying to please others, including my family, that I forget about the most important person: me. I just say yes to everything just to please people.

Then there are the days when the worst things happen. I wish that I could just crawl back in bed for the day and wish the day away. But at the end of the day I hope I do not make the same mistakes again. I try so hard to please my family, and there is nothing I can do. No matter what I do, I am not perfect in their eyes. This makes me think, What do they want from me? But I go on understanding that I cannot please myself all the time, and sometimes it is easier to please everyone else. This song shows me I am not the only one who feels this way.

---

I cannot change the fact that while my mother watched me graduate from basic training in the army, a man we thought was a family friend molested my brother, a crime I have blamed myself for ever since. I cannot change the fact that I wasn't there to stop my good friend from committing suicide, also something I have blamed myself for. I can't change my relationship with my father, who died before I got a chance to mend the rift between us. Thank you for giving me a chance to open these wounds and vent them.

$\mathcal{S}$ometimes, the hardest things to let go of are the things that you have done. I have grown into a very successful person with a loving family and friends who think I'm great, but I still have to look past memories of doing things that I cannot change. I am strong-minded, careful, and respectful, but when I was younger I hurt a lot of people with my lack of care for life. I am disgusted with some of the things I've done, but I'm proud for seeing them and knowing that I'm different now. It is so hard to separate us from our past actions. I know many people have regrets, and I am hopeful that I will feel better about myself the more I prove to myself that I am different.

$\mathcal{W}$hat is often forgotten is that each of us owns the path we walk. It's up to the individual who it's shared with. When you surround yourself with people you love and they love you back, your path becomes a beautiful place to be. Others want to be with you. Remember we have a choice. We own our own path. Ownership is a beautiful thing.

$\mathcal{W}$hen I was younger I battled bulimia for a couple of years. I felt like my life was spinning out of control. I thought I had to be skinny and beautiful for people to love me. I lost myself for a while, but now I am a healthy woman. I am so thankful that I was strong enough to realize what was most important in life and to take care of myself. I changed what I could and let go of trying to please everyone else. Now I please myself, and I feel more beautiful than I ever have.

*Longing to Be Parents*

The thing I cannot change is the fact that I am twenty years old and they want me to have a hysterectomy. I have a rare disorder that causes blood clots, swelling, and severe pain. I have always loved children and have always wanted some of my own. Now I have to make a decision that I don't want to make. I know that I cannot change what is wrong, but I have decided to have the surgery and to be a foster parent and adopt children who cannot change the fact that they were abandoned or who have had something bad happen to their family. Maybe together these children and I can help one another, and I can give them the love and compassion they deserve.

---

Six months ago today I found out my husband and I were having a baby together. This was his biggest dream, to become a dad. His dad had died twenty days before his birth. I'm so happy I can give that to him, although this wasn't my dream. I never imagined having kids of my own. My dream was to adopt. I always thought to myself, Why bring another child into this world when there are so many out there who need families? I'm hoping once our little one comes into the world that my whole perspective on having a baby will change. I fear I won't be a good mom to my own biological child. I know God wouldn't have done it if it weren't meant to be.

*I* have been married for twelve years and have lost six pregnancies. I will never be able to conceive on my own without the help of hormones and heparin injections. Last year we lost a baby at fifteen and a half weeks. We tried again three months later, and I got pregnant. I went into labor, and when the doctors tried to save the pregnancy, my water broke and I lost the baby. My job fired me because I couldn't come into work while I was in the hospital. I lost two baby boys in a year. God is the one who gave me all the strength to get through this trial. I don't know why my husband and I have struggled our whole marriage but we have.

I will learn to let go. God, I will learn to let go. . . .

*M*y husband and I have gone through many years of fertility treatments and none have worked. I met LeAnn about five years ago and told her how her music helps us through the many ups and downs. She got a little teary and told us, "Never lose hope." I have held on to those words and still have never lost hope that we will someday be parents. You blame yourself, others, and you blame God. We have come to accept things more through the lyrics of "What I Cannot Change." It makes you remember to be thankful for each other and the love you share no matter how hard things get.

*I* am thirty-four. I suffered with infertility for two years, and surrendered four angel babies to Heaven's Nursery along the way. This two-year journey to become a mother has challenged me to find grace and acceptance in God's plan, and to learn to love, forgive, and accept all of what I cannot change. I found inspiration, power, strength, healing, and faith through prayer, support, and your music. All of my obstacles, disappointments, losses, and devastation came full circle this past January when I heard my son's first cry, and I looked into his eyes as he grasped my finger in his tiny fist. As I whispered "It was all worth it," I found completion.

*W*hat I cannot change is that parenting is not easy, nor is there a book to learn by, or a class to attend. But I am blessed to have a son who loves me not only for my mistakes, but also because I am able to change and learn for life with him.

# Health

My girlfriend has been fighting a rare form of ovarian cancer for the last three years of our life together. Every day has been a huge struggle, and every day I have had to learn to adapt and love and even to talk to God in a different way. The change is not easy, and I have never dealt well with change. Today we are one step closer to her being free from this cancer. We find out next week if she has anything new forming and we pray to God she does not. And then there will be a new change in our life once again as we start over, so to speak, and the pieces can be put back together for the both of us.

———

This song has changed my life. I am twelve years old and lucky to be here. I have learned that I have an illness called cerebral palsy. It is a disability that affected my right side. I was born at one pound, six ounces on March 11—my real due date was June 30. Anyway, this song changed my life because it has helped me realize that I can't change my life. Sometimes I don't know why I am still here. My parents call me a miracle baby. Before I heard this song I thought they were saying that because they are my parents, but after hearing this song I realize that it's true.

———

For anyone reading this who has a mentally ill loved one, you are in my thoughts and prayers. By listening to the words of your song often I can accept and forgive whatever made my husband mentally ill.

---

I cannot change the feelings I have when it comes to my beautiful special needs daughter. I feel my father and mother don't really have the same relationship with my daughter as they do with my nieces and nephews. Maybe I am looking too much into it, but my daughter is so dear and special to my heart, it just hurts that they don't have a relationship with her. I know they love her dearly. That's not the issue. I just wish they would include her in the family functions like they do the other kids. May God bless all those special needs children in the world who need some encouragement.

---

This song really brings back memories of how my daddy suffered with Parkinson's and Alzheimer's. My mother, God bless her, was an angel through it all. The family had to put him in a nursing home because he was getting too much for my mother to handle. She would go there every day and feed him and talk to him, but Daddy didn't say anything. He was in his own little world. When I would go to see him, it would always bring tears to my eyes because I was Daddy's little girl. He said things about missing all of his grandchildren growing up. I could see it in his eyes; he was so tired but wouldn't let go. I lay beside him one day and said to him, "Daddy, it's okay. We love you so much but you can go, we will be okay." Three days later, Daddy went to Heaven. I lost my buddy then. I wish I could have changed things, but I couldn't. Remember to always tell your parents you love them, because one day they will not be here for you to tell them.

---

*I* cannot change the fact that my mom is slowly and painfully dying of cancer. I can't change that the day I have dreaded all my life is closer every day. I can't change my ex-husband into a decent father and human being. I will learn to let go of the hurt my divorce caused me and my kids. I will learn to forgive those who have hurt me. I will cherish every day with my beautiful kids and wonderful new husband. I will learn to live my life with no regrets. I will make sure my family knows how much I love them. I will treasure every moment with my mom as it may be the last. I will count my blessings every day. I will live each day being the best mom, wife, sister, and friend I can be. I will learn to accept what I cannot change.

---

*I* am thirty-seven years old, and I was born with spina bifida, which means I have an open spine. I was so messed up when I was born that the doctors didn't think I would live a year. Now, almost thirty-eight years and nearly eighty surgeries later, I am still alive and without the help of my mother who hasn't spoken to me since I left home when I was twenty-one. I am now a wife of sixteen years and a mother of a ten-year-old son. I am so blessed with a man who sees past my disability and my crutches, which I have to use around the apartment, and my wheelchair for longer distances. I am a very independent woman who does everything for my husband and our son. I am the wife, mother, maid, teacher, pet keeper, and finder of all lost things. So no matter what people tell you, never give up. Like I tell my son, you can do anything you want in life if you put your mind to it with a little bit of effort. I was with my husband for four years before we got pregnant; then I miscarried. With the love of my husband and God I was pregnant four months later with the son we have now.

***

My son Jeff is now twenty-three years old. He was the funniest, smartest, sweetest kid; he was my "little bubby." Three years ago he was diagnosed a paranoid schizophrenic. The boy I knew is now gone, replaced by a mean, ranting, out-of-control and psychotic person. Not even close to who he once was. I have never felt so much pain and heartache, not even when my mom committed suicide. I've prayed for thousands of hours. As I am writing these words I am crying, knowing he will never get better, and I cannot change that.

# About the Authors

*Le Ann* Rimes first made waves when she was just thirteen years old and her debut single, "Blue," became a national hit. She's scored numerous hit singles since then, among them "One Way Ticket," "I Need You," "Nothin' 'Bout Love Makes Sense," "Probably Wouldn't Be This Way," "Can't Fight the Moonlight"—which was a number one song in eleven countries—and "How Do I Live," which was the longest-running single ever on the Billboard Hot 100, spending a record-setting sixty-nine weeks on the chart.

*Darrell* Brown is an award-winning songwriter, record producer, and arranger. He cowrote the number one hit "You'll Think of Me" by Keith Urban, which won the Grammy Award for Best Male Country Vocal Performance in 2006. Brown has worked with the legends of music, from Willie Dixon to Dolly Parton to Neil Young. Brown cowrote nine of the songs on LeAnn Rimes's newest album, *Family,* and contributes regularly to the *New York Times* online music column "Measure for Measure."

# About the CD

On this CD you will find an unplugged acoustic version of "What I Cannot Change" that LeAnn performed for the radio show *Artist Confidential.* This is the first time this recording, courtesy of XM Radio, has been released. Also included are recordings of LeAnn and her songwriting friend, Darrell, reading their personal stories behind the creation of the song.